POPULAR SONGS
HAL LEONARD
TUDENT PIANO LIBRARY

INTERMEDIATE PIANO SOLOS

Top Hits

Arranged by Jennifer and Mike Watts

ISBN: 978-1-4584-2083-1

7777 W. BLUEMOUND RD. P.O. BOX 13819 MILWAUKEE, WI 53213

Visit Hal Leonard Online at
www.halleonard.com

CONTENTS

4   Every Teardrop Is a Waterfall
      COLDPLAY

12   For the First Time
      THE SCRIPT

19   Jar of Hearts
      CHRISTINA PERRI

26   Just the Way You Are
      BRUNO MARS

34   Rolling in the Deep
      ADELE

40   Someone Like You
      ADELE

48   You and I
      LADY GAGA

Every Teardrop Is a Waterfall

Words and Music by Guy Berryman,
Jon Buckland, Will Champion,
Chris Martin, Peter Allen,
Adrienne Anderson and Brian Eno
Arranged by Jennifer & Mike Watts

Folk Rock (♩ = 112)

With pedal

I turn the mu-sic __ up, __ I've got my

rec-ords __ on, __ I shut the world out-side __ un-til the lights come on. __ May-be the

streets a - light, may-be the trees are __ gone, __ but I feel my heart start __ beat-ing to my

fa - v'rite __ song. __ And all the kids, they __ dance, _ all the kids, all __ night, _ un - til

Mon - day __ mor - ing feels an - oth - er ___ life. __ I turn the mu - sic __ up, __ I'm on a

roll this __ time __ and heav - en __ is in sight. ___

I turn the mu - sic ___ up, ___ I've got my

f

rec - ords ___ on, ___ from un - der - neath the ___ rub - ble, sing a reb - el ___ song. Don't want to

see an - oth - er gen - er - a - tion ___ drop, ___ I'd rath - er be a ___ com - ma than

a full — stop. — May-be I'm in the — black, — may-be I'm on my — knees, — may-be I'm

in the — gap — be-tween the two trap - ez - es. But my heart is — beat - ing and my

puls - es — start — ca - the - drals — in my heart. — As we —

saw, whoa, — this — light, —

I swear you   e - merge, blink - ing, __ in - to, to

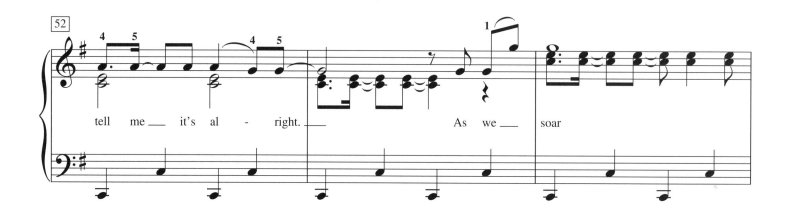

tell me __ it's al - right. __ As we __ soar

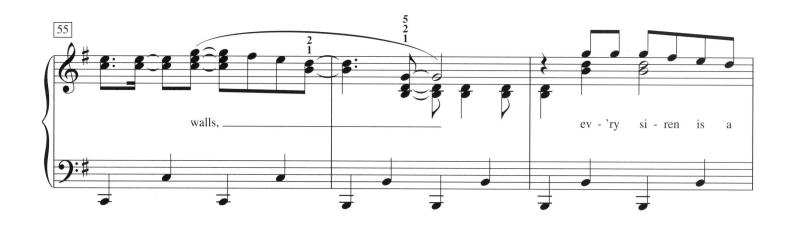

walls, _____ ev - 'ry si - ren is a

sym - pho - ny. __ And ev - 'ry tear's a wa - ter - fall, __

is a wa-ter-fall. Oh, is a wa-ter-fall.

Oh, is a wa-ter-fall. It is, it

is, is a wa-ter-fall. Oh. So you can't hurt,

hurt me bad.

But still I'll raise

the flag.

It was a

wa - ter - fall. __ A wa - ter - fall. __

10

For the First Time

Words and Music by Mark Sheehan
and Daniel O'Donoghue
Arranged by Jennifer & Mike Watts

Moderately slow (♩ = 88)

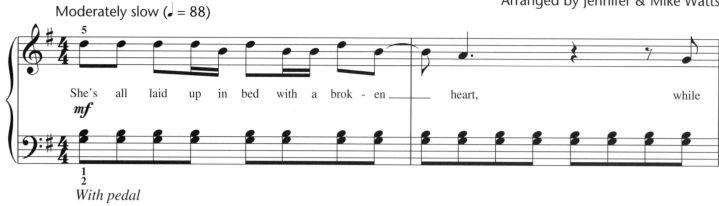

She's all laid up in bed with a brok-en _____ heart, while

I'm drink-in' Jack all a-lone in my lo-cal bar. _____ And we don't know _ how,

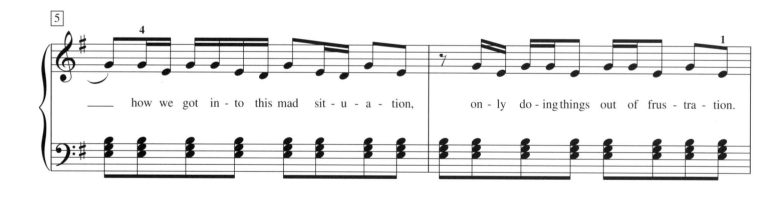

_____ how we got in-to this mad sit-u-a-tion, on-ly do-ing things out of frus-tra-tion.

Try'n' to make it work, but man, _ these times are hard. _____ She

needs me now, __ but I can't seem to find the time. __ I got a
She's in __ line at the door with her head held high, while

new job now __ on the un-em-ploy-ment line. __ And we don't know __ how, __
I just lost my job __ but did-n't lose my pride. And we both know __ how, __

__ how we got in-to this mess. Is it God's test? Some-one help us, 'cause we're do-ing our best.
__ how we're gon-na make it work when it hurts, when you pick your-self __ up, you get __ kicked to the dirt.

Try'n' to make it work, but man, __ these times are hard. __ But we're gon-na start __ by

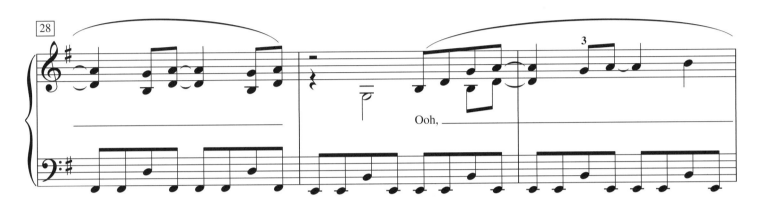

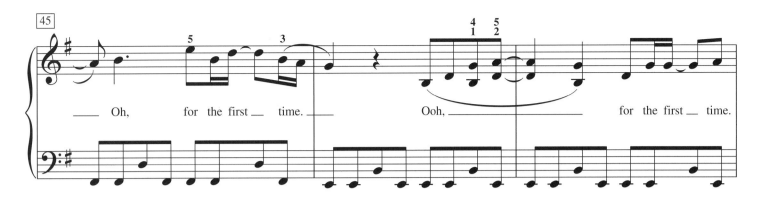

yeah, they're mak - ing us cra - zy. Don't give up on me, ba - by. ___

Oh, these times are hard, ___ yeah, they're mak - ing us cra - zy. Don't give up on me, ba -

- by. ___ Oh, these times are hard, ___ yeah, they're mak - ing us cra -

- zy. Don't give up on me, ba - by. ___

rit.

mp

Jar of Hearts

Words and Music by Barrett Yeretsian,
Christina Perri and Drew Lawrence
Arranged by Jennifer & Mike Watts

Moderate Ballad (♩ = 88)

mp I know I can't take one more ___ step ___ towards ___ you,

With pedal

'cause all that's wait - ing is re - gret. ___

And don't you know I'm not your ___ ghost ___ an - y - more, ___

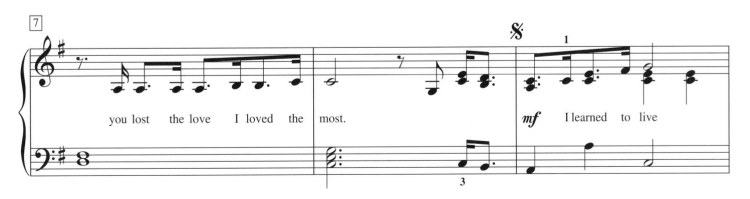

you lost the love I loved the most. *mf* I learned to live

soul. _____ So don't come back for me. Who do you think you are? _

___ I hear you're ask - ing all a - round _

_____ if I am an - y - where to ___ be _

__ found. But I have grown _ too ____ strong _____

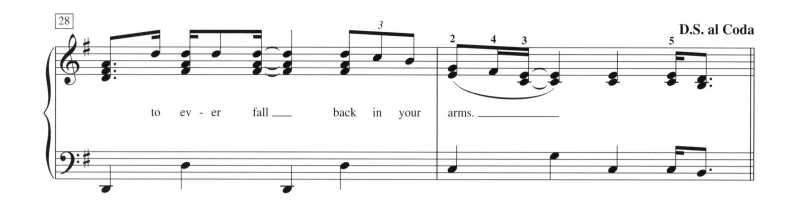

to ev - er fall ___ back in your arms. _____

CODA

___ And it took so long just to

feel al - right, _____ re - mem - ber ___ how to ___ put back the

light in my eyes. _____ I wish I had ___ missed the first ___

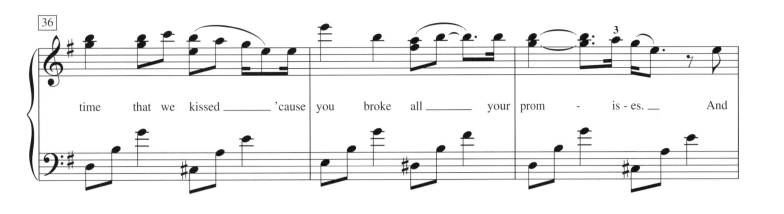

time that we kissed _____ 'cause you broke all _____ your prom - is - es. __ And

now you're back, _ you don't get to get me back. _____

__ And who do you think you are, ___ run - ning 'round leav - ing

scars, _____ col - lect - ing your jar of hearts ___ and tear - ing love a - part? _

You're gon - na catch ___ a cold ___ from the ice in - side ___ your

soul. _____ So don't come back for me, don't come back ___ at

all. _____ And who do you think you are, ___ run - ning 'round ___ leav - ing

scars, _____ col - lect - ing your jar of hearts, _____ tear - ing love a - part? _

You're gon - na catch ___ a cold ___ from the ice in - side ___ your

soul.   Don't come back   for   me,   don't come back   at   all.

Who do   you think   you ___ are?   Who do   you think   you ___

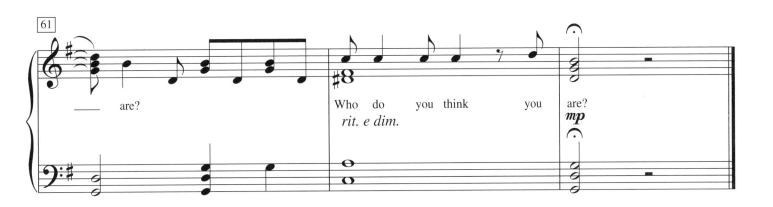

___ are?   Who do   you think   you   are?

rit. e dim.   **mp**

Just the Way You Are

Words and Music by Bruno Mars,
Ari Levine, Philip Lawrence,
Khari Cain and Khalil Walton
Arranged by Jennifer & Mike Watts

per - fect - ly ___ with - out ___ her try - in'. She's so beau - ti - ful, ___

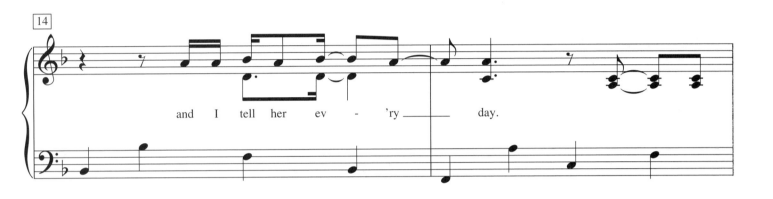

and I tell her ev - 'ry ___ day.

Yeah. I know, ___ I know ___ when I

com - pli - ment _ her, she won't be - lieve _ me. And it's so, ___ it's so ___ sad to

think that she ___ don't see what I ___ see. But ev-'ry time ___ she asks me, "Do ___

___ I look o - kay?" ___ I ___ say:

When I see your face, ___ there's not a thing ___

___ that I ___ would change, ___ 'cause you're a - maz - ing ___ just ___

the way ___ you are. ___ And when you smile, ___

the whole world stops ___ and stares ___ for a while, ___

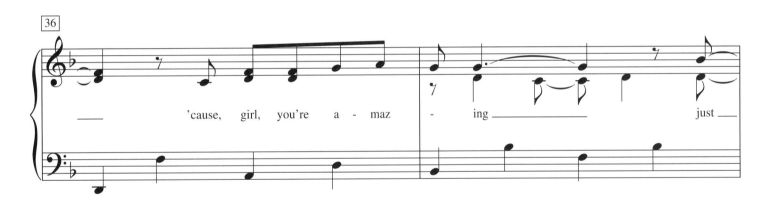

___ 'cause, girl, you're a - maz - ing ___ just ___

To Coda ⊕

___ the way ___ you are. ___ Yeah. ___

Her lips, ___ her lips, ___ I could kiss them all ___ day if ___ she'd let me.

Her laugh, ___ her laugh, ___ she hates but I ___ think it's ___ so sex - y.

She's so beau - ti - ful, ___ and I tell her ev - 'ry ___

___ day. Oh, you know, you know, you know I'd nev - er

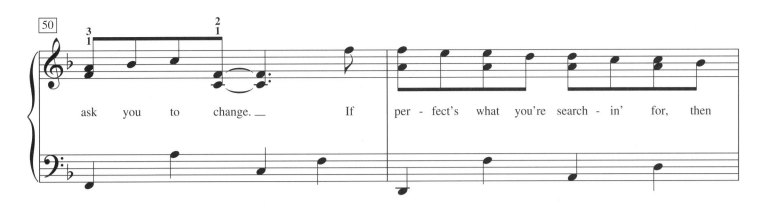

ask you to change. _ If per - fect's what you're search - in' for, then

just stay the same. _ So _ don't e - ven both - er ask - in' if _

_ you look o - kay. _ You know I'll say: _

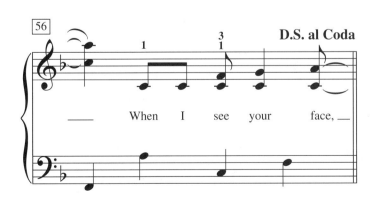

D.S. al Coda

_ When I see your face, _

CODA

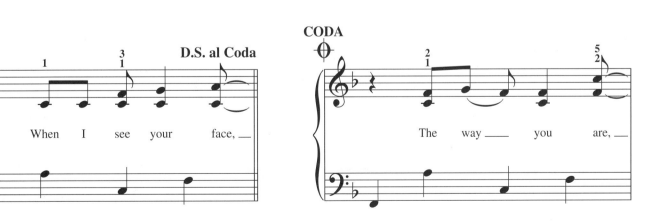

The way _ you are, _

31

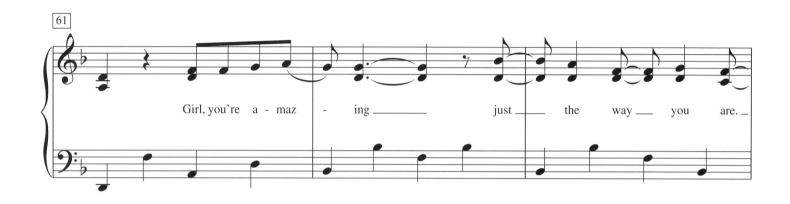

-ing   just ____ the   way ____ you   are. ____

And when you   smile, ____   the whole world   stops ____

____ and   stares ____ for   a   while, ____   'cause, girl, you're a - maz   -   ing   just ____

____ the   way ____ you   are. ____   Yeah. ____

Rolling in the Deep

Words and Music by Adele Adkins
and Paul Epworth
Arranged by Jennifer & Mike Watts

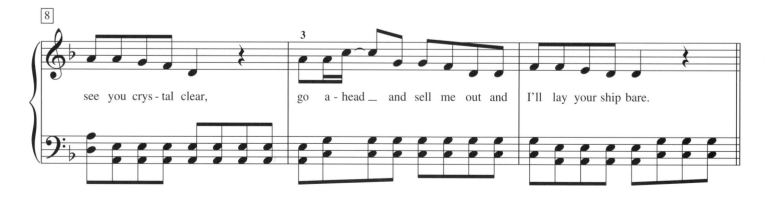

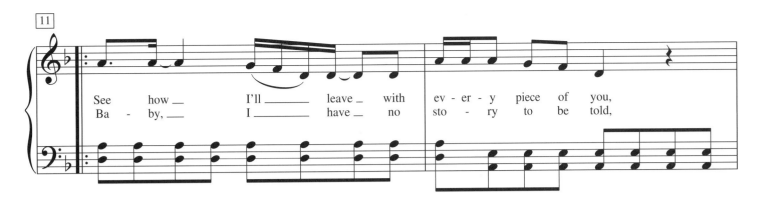

See how — I'll ———— leave — with ev - er - y piece of you,
Ba — by, — I ———— have no sto - ry to be told,

don't un - der - es - ti - mate the things that I ——— will do.
but I've — heard one on you, now I'm gon - na make your head burn.

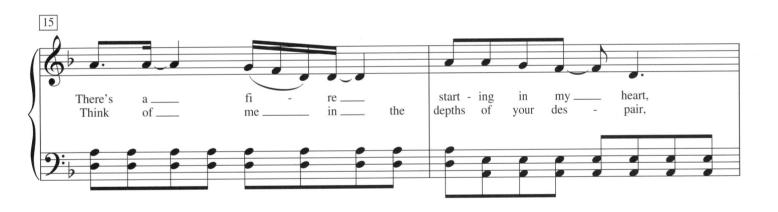

There's a ——— fi - re ——— the start - ing in my ——— heart,
Think of ——— me ———— in ——— the depths of your des - pair,

reach - ing ——— a fe - ver pitch and it's bring - ing me out the dark. —
make a ———— home down there as ——— mine sure ——— won't be shared. —

The scars of your ___ love re-mind me of ___ us. They keep me

think-ing that we al-most had it all. The scars of

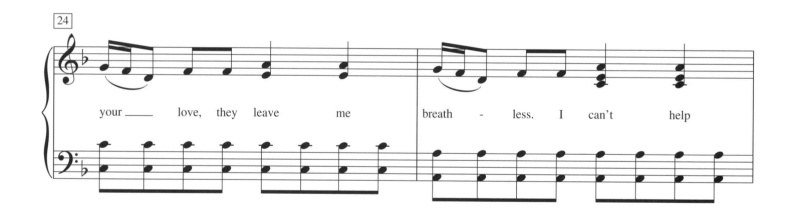

your ___ love, they leave me breath-less. I can't help

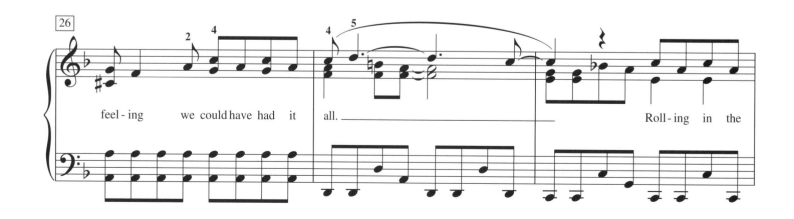

feel-ing we could have had it all. ___ Roll-ing in the

deep. _____ You had my heart in - side _____ of your hand, _

_____ and you played ____ it ____ to the beat. _____

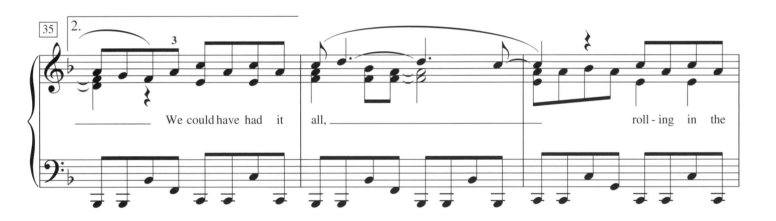

_____ We could have had it all, _____ roll - ing in the

deep. _____ You had my heart in - side _____ of your hand _

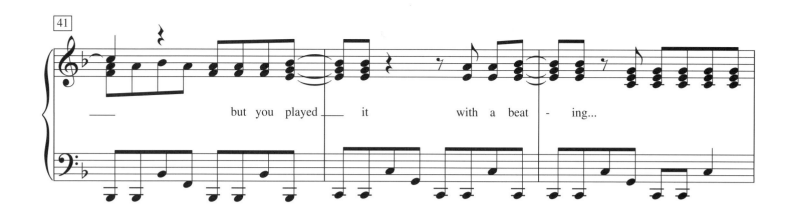

but you played ___ it with a beat - ing...

Throw your ___ soul ___ through ev-er-y o-pen door, count your ___ bless - ings to

find what you look for. Turn my sor - rows in - to treas-ured gold. You'll

pay me ___ back in kind and reap just what you could have had it

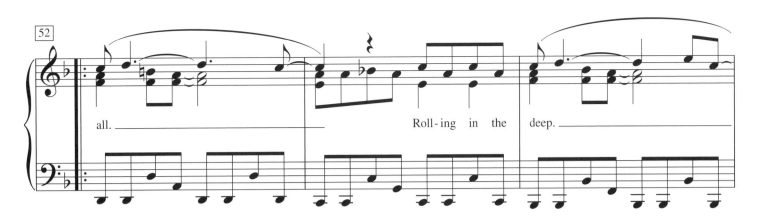

all. _____ Roll-ing in the deep. _____

_____ You had my heart in - side _____ of your hand, _

_____ and you played ___ it to the beat. _____ We could have had it

_____ it, you played _ it, you played ___ it, you played _ it to the beat. _____

Someone Like You

Words and Music by Adele Adkins
and Dan Wilson
Arranged by Jennifer & Mike Watts

Piano Ballad (♩ = 60)

With pedal

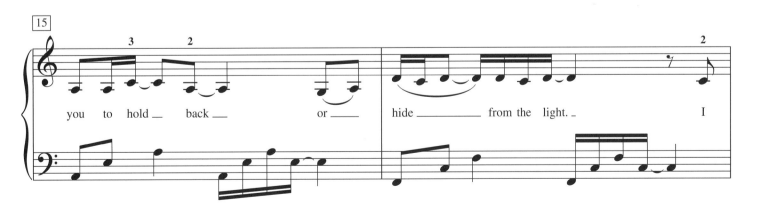

hate to turn up ___ out of the blue un - in - vit - ed, but I ___ could-n't stay a - way, ___ I could-n't fight it. I had

hoped you'd see my face ___ and that you'd be re - mind - ed that, for ___ me, _____ it is - n't o - ver. ___

Nev - er mind, ___ I'll ___ find ___ some - one like ___

___ you. _____ I wish noth-ing but ___ the best ___ for ___ you, ___ too. Don't for-

get me, I beg. __ I __ re - mem - ber __ you said, __ "Some - times it

lasts in love, but some - times it hurts in - stead." Some - times it

lasts in love, but some - times it hurts in - stead. __

__ You __ know __ how __ the

mp

time flies, ___ on - ly ___ yes - ter - day ___ was the

time of our lives. We ___ were born and raised ___ in a

sum - mer haze, bound by the sur - prise of our

glo - ry ___ days. I hate to turn up ___ out of the blue un - in - vit - ed, but I ___

could-n't stay a-way, __ I could-n't fight it. I had hoped you'd see my face and that you'd be re-mind-ed that, for

D.S. al Coda

me, __ it is-n't o - ver. __

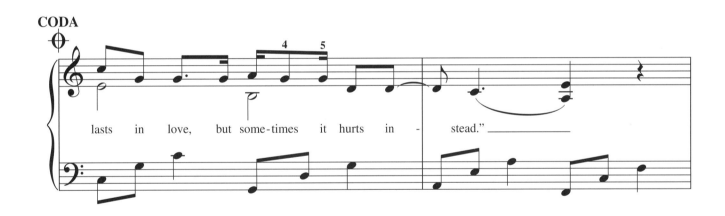

CODA

lasts in love, but some-times it hurts in-stead." __

Noth-ing com-pares, no wor-ries or cares, re - grets and mis-takes, they're mem - o - ries made.

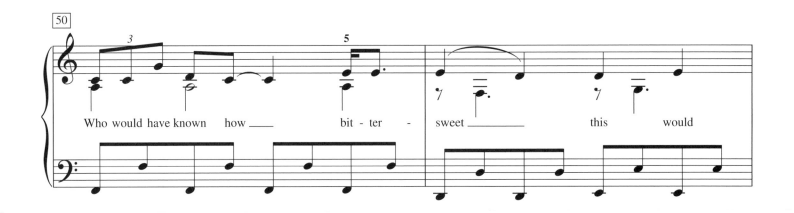

Who would have known how ____ bit - ter - sweet _____ this would

taste?
rit.

Nev - er mind, _ I'll _ find _ some-one like _
a tempo

__ you. _____ I wish noth-ing but _ the best _ for _ you, ___ too. Don't for-

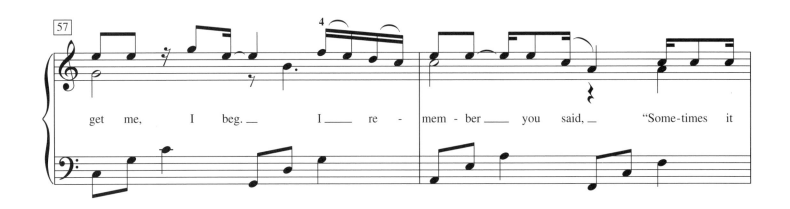

get me, I beg. __ I re - mem - ber ___ you said, _ "Some-times it

lasts in love, but some-times it hurts in - stead."

- stead." Some-times it lasts in love, but some-times it hurts in -

- stead.

mp   *p*

rit.

Yoü and I

Words and Music by
Stefani Germanotta
Arranged by Jennifer & Mike Watts

Power Ballad (♩ = 60) Swing 16ths

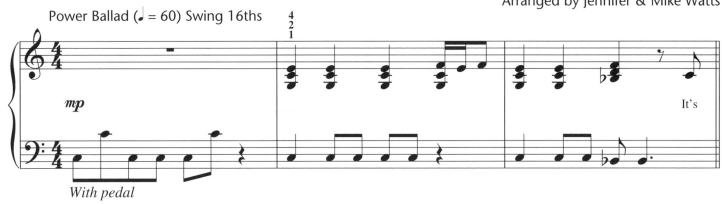

It's

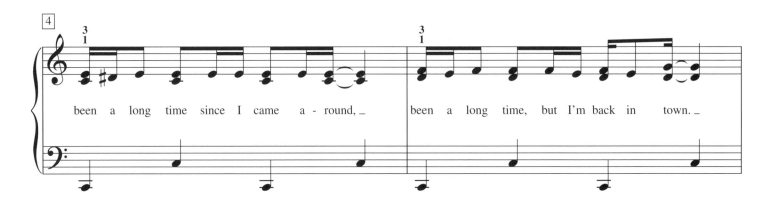

been a long time since I came a- round, __ been a long time, but I'm back in town. __

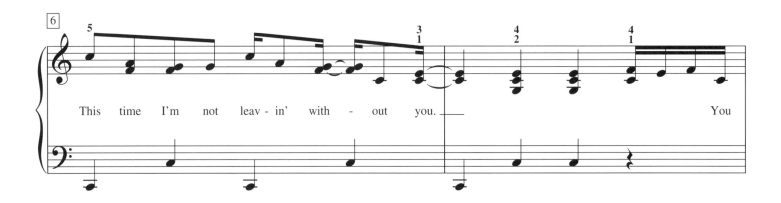

This time I'm not leav- in' with- out you. ____ You

taste like whis-key when you kiss me, __ oh. __ I'd give an- y-thing a- gain to be your ba- by doll.

This time I'm not leav - in' with - out you. _____ He said,

"Sit back down where _ you be - long, _ in the cor - ner of my bar with your high heels on.

Sit back down on the couch where we _____ made love the first time." And you said to me _____ there's

some-thin', some-thin' a - bout _ this place. _____ Some-thin' a-bout lone-ly nights _ and my

On my birth-day you sang me __ "Heart of __ Gold" __ with a

gui - tar __ hum-min' and __ no clothes. __ This time I'm not leav - in' with - out

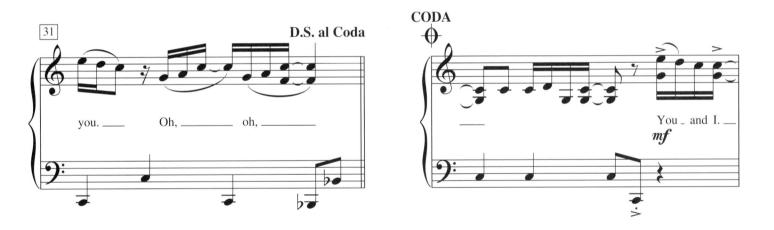

D.S. al Coda

CODA

you. __ Oh, __ oh, __

__ You _ and I. __

mf

You, you _ and I. __ You, you _ and I. __ You, you _ and

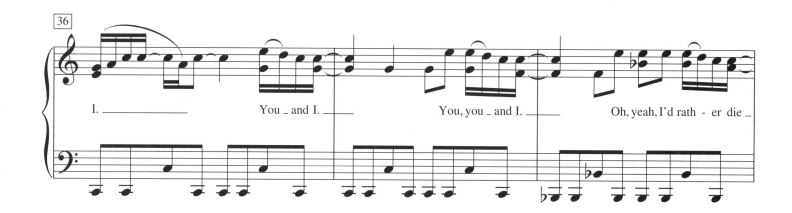

I._____ You _ and I. _____ You, you _ and I. _____ Oh, yeah, I'd rath - er die _

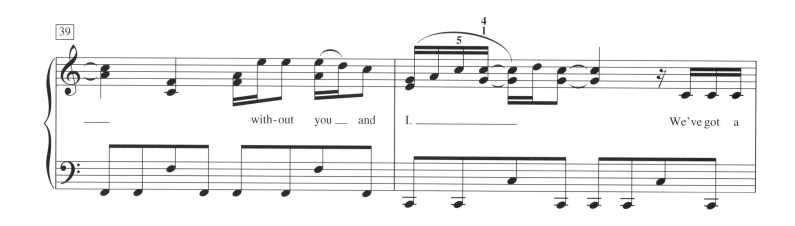

_____ with-out you _ and I. _____ We've got a

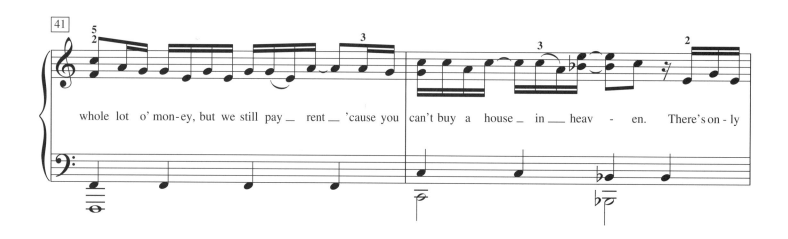

whole lot o' mon-ey, but we still pay _ rent _ 'cause you can't buy a house _ in _ heav - en. There's on - ly

three men that I'm - a serve in my whole life: _ it's my dad-dy and Ne-bras-ka and _ Je - sus _ Christ. _ There's

some-thin', some-thin' a-bout the chase. I'm a

New York wom-an, born to run you down. So, want my lip-stick all o-ver your face?

Some-thin', some-thin' a-bout just know-in' when it's right. So put your

drinks up for Ne-bras-ka, for Ne-bras-ka, Ne-bras-ka, I love ya. You and I.

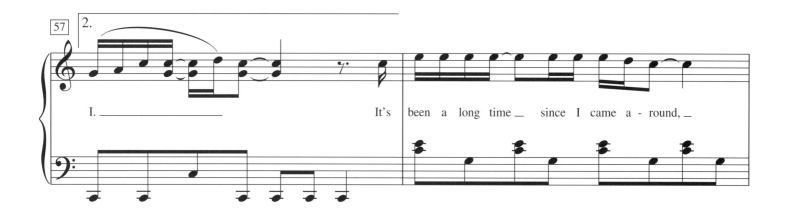

The **Hal Leonard Student Piano Library** has great songs, and you will find all your favorites here: Disney classics, Broadway and movie favorites, and today's top hits. These graded collections are skillfully and imaginatively arranged for students and pianists at every level, from elementary solos with teacher accompaniments to sophisticated piano solos for the advancing pianist.

The Beatles
arr. Eugénie Rocherolle
Intermediate piano solos. Songs: *Can't Buy Me Love • Get Back • Here Comes the Sun • Martha My Dear • Michelle • Ob-La-Di, Ob-La-Da • Revolution • Yesterday.*
00296649 Correlates with HLSPL Level 5.........$10.99

Irving Berlin Piano Duos
arr. Don Heitler and Jim Lyke
Beautiful duo arrangements for two pianos, four hands. Two scores are included: *Cheek to Cheek • They Say It's Wonderful • (I Wonder Why?) You're Just in Love.*
00296838 Correlates with HLSPL Level 5........$14.99

Broadway Hits
arr. Carol Klose
Early-Intermediate/Intermediate piano solos. Songs: *Beauty and the Beast • Circle of Life • Do-Re-Mi • It's a Grand Night for Singing • The Music of the Night • Tomorrow • Where Is Love? • You'll Never Walk Alone.*
00296650 Correlates with HLSPL Levels 4/5 .....$7.99

Chart Hits
arr. Mona Rejino
8 pop favorites carefully arranged at an intermediate level. Songs: *Bad Day • Boston • Everything • February Song • Home • How to Save a Life • Put Your Records On • What Hurts the Most.*
00296710 Correlates with HLSPL Level 5......... $7.99

Christmas Cheer
arr. Phillip Keveren
Early Intermediate level. For 1 Piano/4 Hands. Songs: *Caroling, Caroling • The Christmas Song • It Must Have Been the Mistletoe • It's Beginning to Look like Christmas • Rudolph the Red-Nosed Reindeer • You're All I Want for Christmas.*
00296616 Correlates with HLSPL Level 4...........$6.95

Christmas Time Is Here
arr. Eugénie Rocherolle
Intermediate level. For 1 piano/4 hands. Songs: *Christmas Time Is Here • Feliz Navidad • Here Comes Santa Claus (Right Down Santa Claus Lane) • I'll Be Home for Christmas • Little Saint Nick • White Christmas.*
00296614 Correlates with HLSPL Level 5...........$7.99

Classic Joplin Rags
arr. Fred Kern
Intermediate/Late Intermediate. Six quintessential Joplin rags arranged by Fred Kern: *Bethena (Concert Waltz) • The Entertainer • Maple Leaf Rag • Pineapple Rag • Pleasant Moments (Ragtime Waltz) • Swipesy (Cake Walk).*
00296743 Correlates with HLSPL Level 5......... $6.95

Contemporary Movie Hits
arr. by Carol Klose, Jennifer Linn and Wendy Stevens
Six blockbuster movie favorites arranged for intermediate-level piano solo: *Bella's Lullaby • Breaking Free • Dawn • Georgiana • He's a Pirate • That's How You Know.*
00296780 Correlates with HLSPL Level 5..........$8.99

Contemporary Pop Hits
arr. Wendy Stevens
Seven top hits your late elementary students will love to learn! Includes: *All the Right Moves • Baby • Breakout • Hey, Soul Sister • Love Story • Lovebug • When I Look at You.*
00296836 Correlates with HLSPL Level 3........ $8.99

Country Favorites
arr. Mona Rejino
Nine great country songs: *Always on My Mind • Crazy • God Bless the U.S.A. • Grandpa (Tell Me 'Bout the Good Old Days) • Hey, Good Lookin' • I Will Always Love You • It Was Almost like a Song • Mammas Don't Let Your Babies Grow up to Be Cowboys • Rocky Top.*
00296861 Correlates with HLSPL Level 5.......... $9.99

Current Hits
arr. Mona Rejino
Seven of today's hottest hits by artists such as Coldplay, Daughtry and Leona Lewis arranged as intermediate solos. Includes: *Apologize • Bleeding Love • Bubbly • Love Song • No One • Viva La Vida • What About Now.*
00296768 Correlates with HLSPL Level 5.......... $8.99

Disney Favorites
arr. Phillip Keveren
Late-Elementary/Early-Intermediate piano solos. Songs: *Beauty and the Beast • Circle of Life • A Dream Is a Wish Your Heart Makes • I'm Late; Little April Shower • A Whole New World (Aladdin's Theme) • You Can Fly! • You'll Be in My Heart.*
00296647 Correlates with HLSPL Levels 3/4 .....$9.99

Disney Film Favorites
arr. Mona Rejino
Intermediate arrangements of eight beloved Disney classics: *Cruella De Vil • Friend like Me • Go the Distance • God Help the Outcasts • Scales and Arpeggios • True Love's Kiss • When She Loved Me • You Are the Music in Me.*
00296809 Correlates with HLSPL Level 5....... $10.99

Getting to Know You – Rodgers & Hammerstein Favorites
Illustrated music book. Elementary/Late Elementary piano solos with teacher accompaniments. Songs: *Bali H'ai • Dites-Moi (Tell Me Why) • The Farmer and the Cowman • Getting to Know You • Happy Talk • I Whistle a Happy Tune • I'm Gonna Wash That Man Right Outa My Hair • If I Loved You • Oh, What a Beautiful Mornin' • Oklahoma • Shall We Dance? • Some Enchanted Evening • The Surrey with the Fringe on Top.*
00296613 Correlates with HLSPL Level 3 ....$12.95

Glee
arr. Jennifer Linn
Jennifer Linn provides intermediate-level solo arrangments of seven favorites from *Glee*: *Don't Stop Believin' • Endless Love • Imagine • Jump • Lean on Me • Proud Mary • True Colors.*
00296834 Correlates with HLSPL Level 5 ....$10.99

Elton John
arr. Carol Klose
8 classic Elton John songs arranged as intermediate solos: *Can You Feel the Love Tonight • Candle in the Wind • Crocodile Rock • Goodbye Yellow Brick Road • Sorry Seems to Be the Hardest Word • Tiny Dancer • Written in the Stars • Your Song.*
00296721 Correlates with HLSPL Level 5 ....$8.99

Joplin Ragtime Duets
arr. Fred Kern
Features full-sounding, intermediate-level arrangements for one piano, four hands of: *Heliotrope Bouquet • Magnetic March • Peacherine Rag • The Ragtime Dance.*
00296771 Correlates with HLSPL Level 5.......... $7.99

Jerome Kern Classics
arr. Eugénie Rocherolle
Intermediate level. Students young and old will relish these sensitive stylings of enduring classics: *All the Things You Are • Bill • Can't Help Lovin' Dat Man • I've Told Ev'ry Little Star • The Last Time I Saw Paris • Make Believe • Ol' Man River • Smoke Gets in Your Eyes • The Way You Look Tonight • Who?*
00296577 Correlates with HLSPL Level 5....... $12.99

Movie Favorites
arr. Fred Kern
Early-Intermediate/Intermediate piano solos. Songs: *Forrest Gump (Feather Theme) • Hakuna Matata • My Favorite Things • My Heart Will Go On • The Phantom of the Opera • Puttin' On the Ritz • Stand by Me.*
00296648 Correlates with HLSPL Levels 4/5 .....$7.99

Sing to the King
arr. Phillip Keveren
These expressive arrangements of popular contemporary Christian hits will inspire and delight intermediate-level pianists. Songs include: *By Our Love • Everlasting God • In Christ Alone • Revelation Song • Sing to the King • Your Name • and more.*
00296808 Correlates with HLSPL Level 5.......... $8.99

Sounds of Christmas (Volume 3)
arr. Rosemary Barrett Byers
Late Elementary/Early Intermediate level. For 1 piano/4 hands. Songs: *Blue Christmas • Christmas Is A-Comin' (May God Bless You) • I Saw Mommy Kissing Santa Claus • Merry Christmas, Darling • Shake Me I Rattle (Squeeze Me I Cry) • Silver Bells.*
00296615 Correlates with HLSPL Levels 3/4 .....$7.99

Today's Hits
arr. Mona Rejino
Intermediate-level piano solos. Songs: *Bless the Broken Road • Breakaway • Don't Know Why • Drops of Jupiter (Tell Me) • Home • Listen to Your Heart • She Will Be Loved • A Thousand Miles.*
00296646 Correlates with HLSPL Level 5...........$7.99

Top Hits
arr. Jennifer and Mike Watts
Eight red-hot intermediate top hits: *Every Teardrop Is A Waterfall • For the First Time • Good Life • Jar of Hearts • Just the Way You Are • Rolling In the Deep • Someone Like You • You and I.*
00296894 Correlates with HLSPL Level 5........ $10.99

You Raise Me Up
arr. Deborah Brady
Contemporary Christian favorites. Elementary-level arrangements. Songs: *All I Need • Forever • Open the Eyes of My Heart, Lord • We Bow Down • You Are So Good to Me • You Raise Me Up.*
00296576 Correlates with HLSPL Levels 2/3 .....$7.95

HAL•LEONARD®
CORPORATION

7777 W. BLUEMOUND RD. P.O. BOX 13819 MILWAUKEE, WI 53213

Visit our web site at **www.halleonard.com/hlspl.jsp** for all the newest titles in this series and other books in the Hal Leonard Student Piano Library.

Prices, contents and availability subject to change without notice. Prices may vary outside the U.S.

0512

Hal Leonard Student Piano Library

A piano method with music to please students, teachers and parents!
The **Hal Leonard Student Piano Library** is clear, concise and carefully graded. Perfect for private and group instruction.

Piano Lessons 1-5
Appealing music introduces new concepts

Piano Lessons Instrumental Accompaniments 1-5
Correlated audio CD or General MIDI disk for lessons and games books

Piano Practice Games 1-4
Listening, reading, and improvisation activities correlated with lessons book

Notespeller for Piano 1-3
Note recognition activities

Piano Theory Workbook 1-5
Written theory activities correlated with lessons book

Piano Technique Book 1-5
Etudes to develop physical mastery of the keyboard (Instrumental Accompaniments optional)

Piano Solos 1-5
Additional correlated repertoire (Instrumental Accompaniments optional)

FOR MORE INFORMATION, SEE YOUR LOCAL MUSIC DEALER, OR WRITE TO:

HAL•LEONARD®
CORPORATION
7777 W. BLUEMOUND RD. P.O. BOX 13819 MILWAUKEE, WI 53213

Visit us online at **www.halleonard.com/hlspl.jsp**

0705

Book 1
Piano Lessons
Piano Lessons CD
Piano Lessons GM Disk
Piano Practice Games
Piano Technique Book
Piano Technique CD
Piano Technique GM Disk
Piano Theory Workbook
Piano Solos
Piano Solos CD
Piano Solos GM Disk
Notespeller for Piano
Flash Cards Set A

Book 2
Piano Lessons
Piano Lessons CD
Piano Lessons GM Disk
Piano Practice Games
Piano Technique Book
Piano Technique CD
Piano Technique GM Disk
Piano Theory Workbook
Piano Solos
Piano Solos CD
Piano Solos GM Disk
Notespeller for Piano
Flash Cards Set A

Book 3
Piano Lessons
Piano Lessons CD
Piano Lessons GM Disk
Piano Practice Games
Piano Technique Book
Piano Technique CD
Piano Technique GM Disk
Piano Theory Workbook
Piano Solos
Piano Solos CD
Piano Solos GM Disk
Notespeller for Piano
Flash Cards Set B

Book 4
Piano Lessons
Piano Lessons CD
Piano Lessons GM Disk
Piano Practice Games
Piano Technique Book
Piano Technique CD
Piano Technique GM Disk
Piano Theory Workbook
Piano Solos
Piano Solos CD
Piano Solos GM Disk
Flash Cards Set B

Book 5
Piano Lessons
Piano Lessons CD
Piano Lessons GM Disk
Piano Technique Book
Piano Technique CD
Piano Technique GM Disk
Piano Theory Workbook
Piano Solos
Piano Solos CD
Piano Solos GM Disk

Supplementary
Teacher's Guide & Planning Chart
My Music Journal
Flash Cards Set A
Flash Cards Set B